MODERN AMERICAN HAIKU

Robb Hasencamp

Illustrations by Phillippa Francq

MODERN AMERICAN HAIKU

Robb Hasencamp

Illustrations by Phillippa Francq

MODERN AMERICAN HAIKU

Copyright © 2024 by Robb Hasencamp

ISBN: 978-1962497459 (hc)

ISBN: 978-1962497442 (sc)

ISBN: 978-1962497466 (e)

All rights reserved. No part of this publication may be reproduced, distributed, or transmitted in any form or by any means, including photocopying, recording, or other electronic or mechanical methods, without the prior written permission of the publisher and/or the author, except in the case of brief quotations embodied in critical reviews and other noncommercial uses permitted by copyright law.

The views expressed in this book are solely those of the author and do not necessarily reflect the views of the publisher, and the publisher hereby disclaims any responsibility for them.

The Reading Glass Books
(888) 420-3050
www.readingglassbooks.com
fulfillment@readingglassbooks.com

FOREWORD

Traditional Japanese haiku is poetry based on a rigid format of three lines of 5/7/5 syllables. It typically focuses on nature, deep emotion, and the mysteries of life. Rhyme and rhythm are not employed as has been in traditional American verse. Other elements include contrast, colorful imagery, simplicity, intensity, direct expression, and a feeling of lightness. While Japanese haiku reached its apex in the seventeenth century with Matsuo Basho, the past three hundred years have witnessed an evolution into a Western modernism resembling free verse.

Modern American haiku saw its heyday in the early to midtwentieth century, beginning with Ezra Pound. Allen Ginsburg and Jack Kerouac, in the midcentury, represent a group of Beat and experimental poets who felt that the strict rules of Japanese haiku limited free expression, creativity, and the exploration of expanded subject matter. A host of other remarkable haiku poets have followed this modern Western trend into the late twentieth-century mainstream.

Nonetheless, similarities consist in the three-line (also two-line) format, images of nature, self-knowledge, and a fundamental fascination with brief, discrete moments in time. Again, rhyme and rhythm are eschewed as are other typical poetic mannerisms. The reader is expected to explore a haiku poem seeking deeper meaning that issues from a final, contrasting line of sudden enlightenment.

This present collection of modern American haiku was composed over a two-year period during which I spent vacation time at my sister's cabin in the hills of Tennessee, often went fishing, recalled my many cats' adventures, pondered nature and politics, and other curious truths sent to me in haiku form. The six haiku categories presented here, therefore, cover a variety of subjects that I trust the reader will find both pleasurable and compelling.

BOUNTIFUL NATURE

Tassels toss in breeze
while bees calmly sip
and ants graw at roots

Orange is the color
of this splendid fall day
leaves gathering at queue

Thin yellow light
touches deer's timid tail
a rich primordial glow

Big boulders creek-side wet
glistening with moss
salamander preens in early day

Walking to pond
   a rush of great wings as
heron flaps up through pines

Mother moose drips vegetation
   while son treads
      to keep up

Deep dark mountains
Tennessee woodlands glorious
   in the waning day

Cardinal grooms/on wooden porch rail/that all may know

Dark night
   almost conceals
the lonely palm

Woman wails at end of lake
   then silence, swoosh of wings
   as Loon sails over lonely canoe

Courting dragonflies
alight on tip of fly rod
   ancient love

Rain bubbles plopping
on still waters peaceable lake
   dragonfly awaits

Sunset at pond/sends orange shafts creeping/through the forest

Spreading red barn
nestled in river valley
milk cows all over the place

Ravenous alpha chick
bumps wee owl
over the side

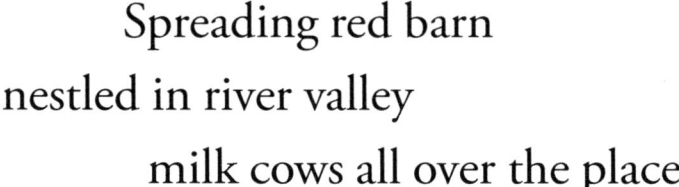

Heron in creek
stabs at crawfish, bream, minnows
a gourmet meal

Palms trees
shiver and howl in the gale
as if all were well

White daisies render joy
petals search for sun
where two souls meet

On wintry night
milk cows stamp, snort
and cuddle close

Pelicans glide silently
in winged formation
eyeing the waves

Leaves aren't turning yet
but the precient, misty chill
is upon us

Billowing cumulus
   against deep blue sky
      seagull soars

Storm on the ridge
     building for deluge
call the animals

Spring ushers in
the astonishing reign
    of butterflies

Autumn dawn
and it appears the mist
may just remain

GAZING AT TRUTH

From balcony on high
park trees blanket beneath where
needles hide with girls

Lovely woman
walks barefoot on pool railing
  please leave her alone

 Again the children —
hundreds of land mines
     lusting for sweet feet

   Thin duck waddles by
with fishing line wrapped
around its beak

Wrong is the color
spewed into helpless waters
our pristine land

We watch as wild beasts
adopt young of natural prey
and are not surprised.

Red Tide rolls in
suffocating all the little ones
oh—the stench!

Glory in Vietnam rain forests
home to rooster, hairy hogs and tiger
blistering death

Three men posing as men
astride old wooden boat
see the muscles!

Some people say/guns don't kill/it's the trigger

Agent Orange fed millions
 but the sappy mist
killed plenty

Out café window
 pretty trees, bright condos, pacing man
 with no name

What's the use
when all she does ends up
inexorable

Apartments stare vacantly
leering from tiny windows
devils' masks in a row

Wildfires sweep the land
no hope in boiling flames
Lady Bug on windshield

Trees crash in the forest
unknown to us out here
inside known to all

Vietnam's crystalline beaches
convey eternal peace
pocked mountains elsewhere

Mother of nine/washes paper dishes/in bronze water

Our civic life
 is a raucous palette
of shameful colors

  Streets in the project
 are fresh and sweet
  moments before dawn

  Hibernating bear
 pushes nose through den wall
  into faltering, foul air

Pastor says female character
is revealed by makeup—
what then of men?

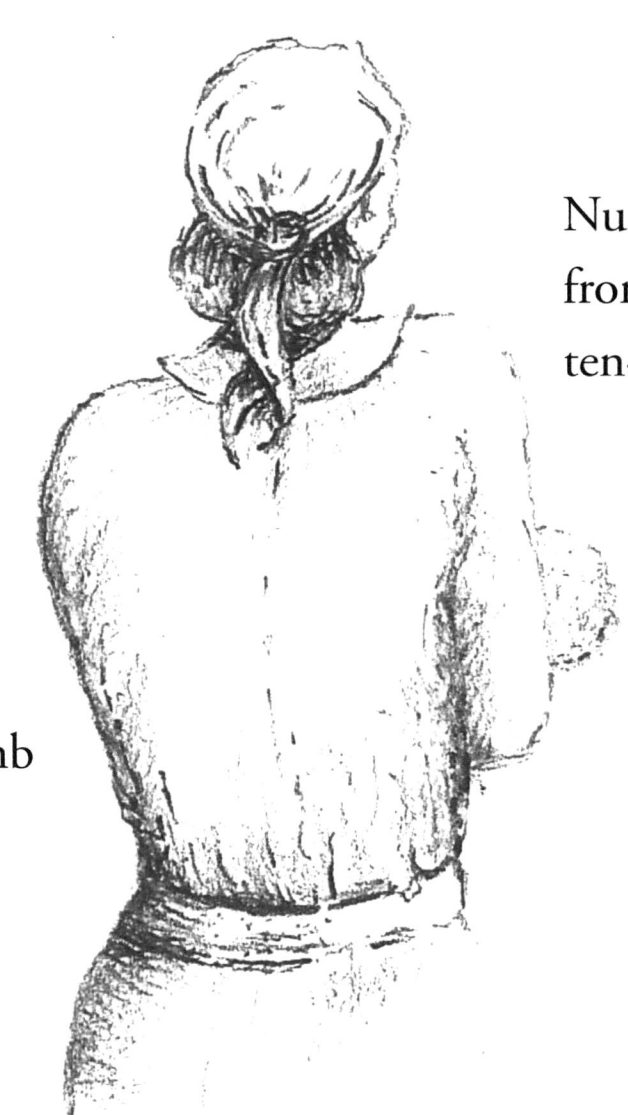

Nurse takes still infant
from mother's arms—
ten-thousand-yard stare

Bob was planning to bomb
an abortion clinic—
then he met Jesus

FUNDAMENTAL FISH

Fishing for bass in pond
    while gloomy rain drizzles
down my beard

No frogs today
so big bass hunts
plump worms

When to set the hook
    so that fish doesn't choke
        takes skill, and tenderness

Fly line curls with grace
    over river laden with trout—
        skunk observes

Manatee gulps at shrimp
   and lumbers steadily off
limp line unfurls

   Silent waters pooling
     deep, sounding aquamarine
       trout watches below

Dragonfly motionless
    perches on taut fishing line
     a fish! and he's away!

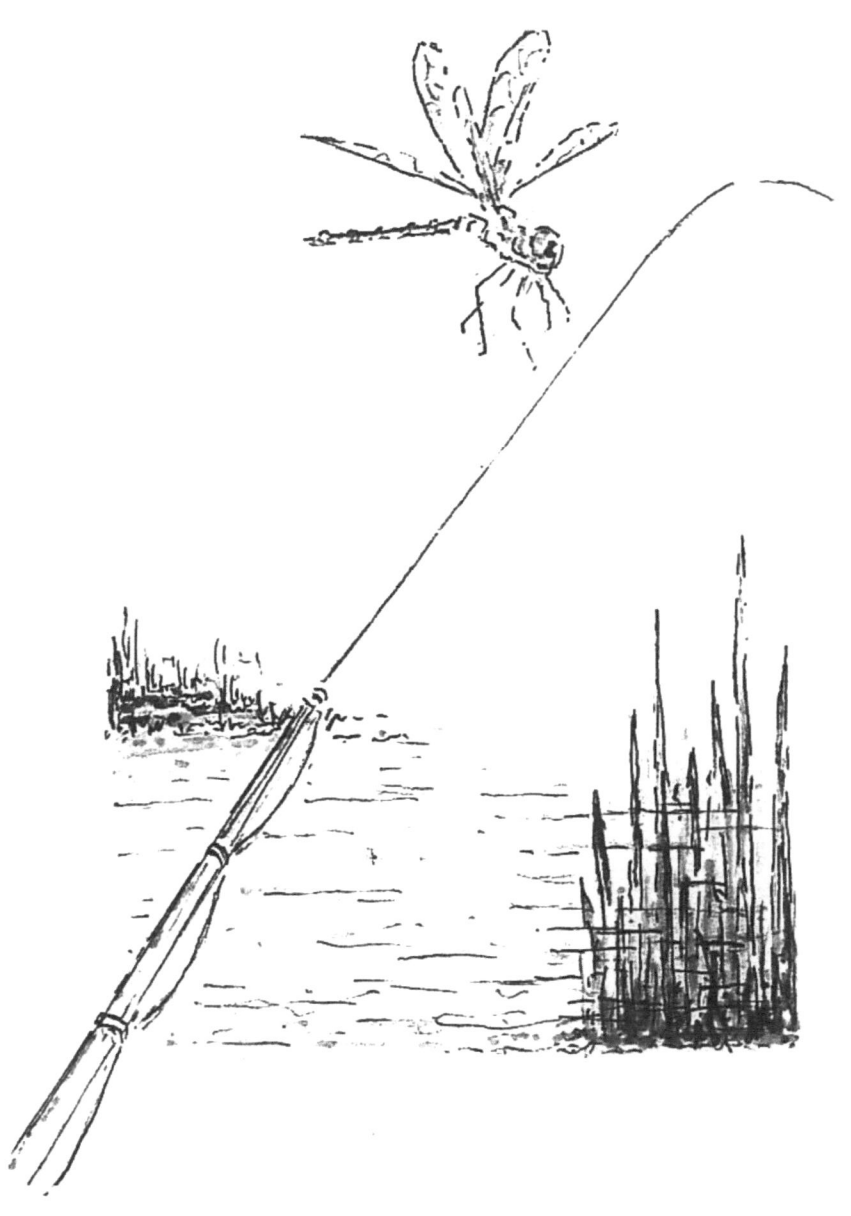

Baby barracuda
    suspended, stalks wee fish
        I blink—see his teeth!

Shark fin like scythe
    carves through calm waters
        seeking the mackerel

Ripples in pond
    make me wonder—my bass?
        nephew arrives with another stone

Blue gills nip at the breadcrumbs
and pose in sharp sunlight
big bass explodes

Bug-eyed bass follows lure/opens maw/that could house ten frogs

Buddy waits on fishing dock
    for my arrival—jaunty trip
        to Ten Thousand Islands

Sly trout treads water
    awaiting tiny ripple
        lifts slowly to kiss

Mullet blast skyward
waters burst sparkling shards
tarpon twists in sun

Fishing cap tilted just so
   I lean against the motor
waiting for big bite

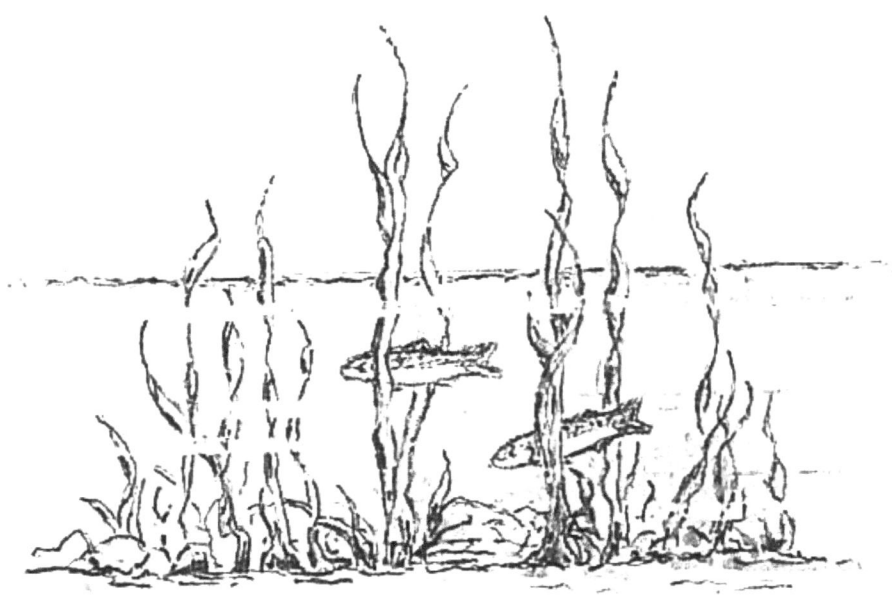

Catfish swallows hook—
   no more rummaging
     the bottom for food

Low water in little brook/feeds shallow pond to nourish/all the bitty fishes

Seaweed gathers at my thighs
tiny shrimp and crabs go about
   as if all were well

Courting dragonflies
   alight on tip of fishing rod
ancient dance of love

Black blue gills/hide in pond's dark shadows/too hot to hunt

Overgrown creek of hairy vines
    hides small trout
     and two yellow boots

Women don't hook worms
    they twist and squirm
      feeling pain

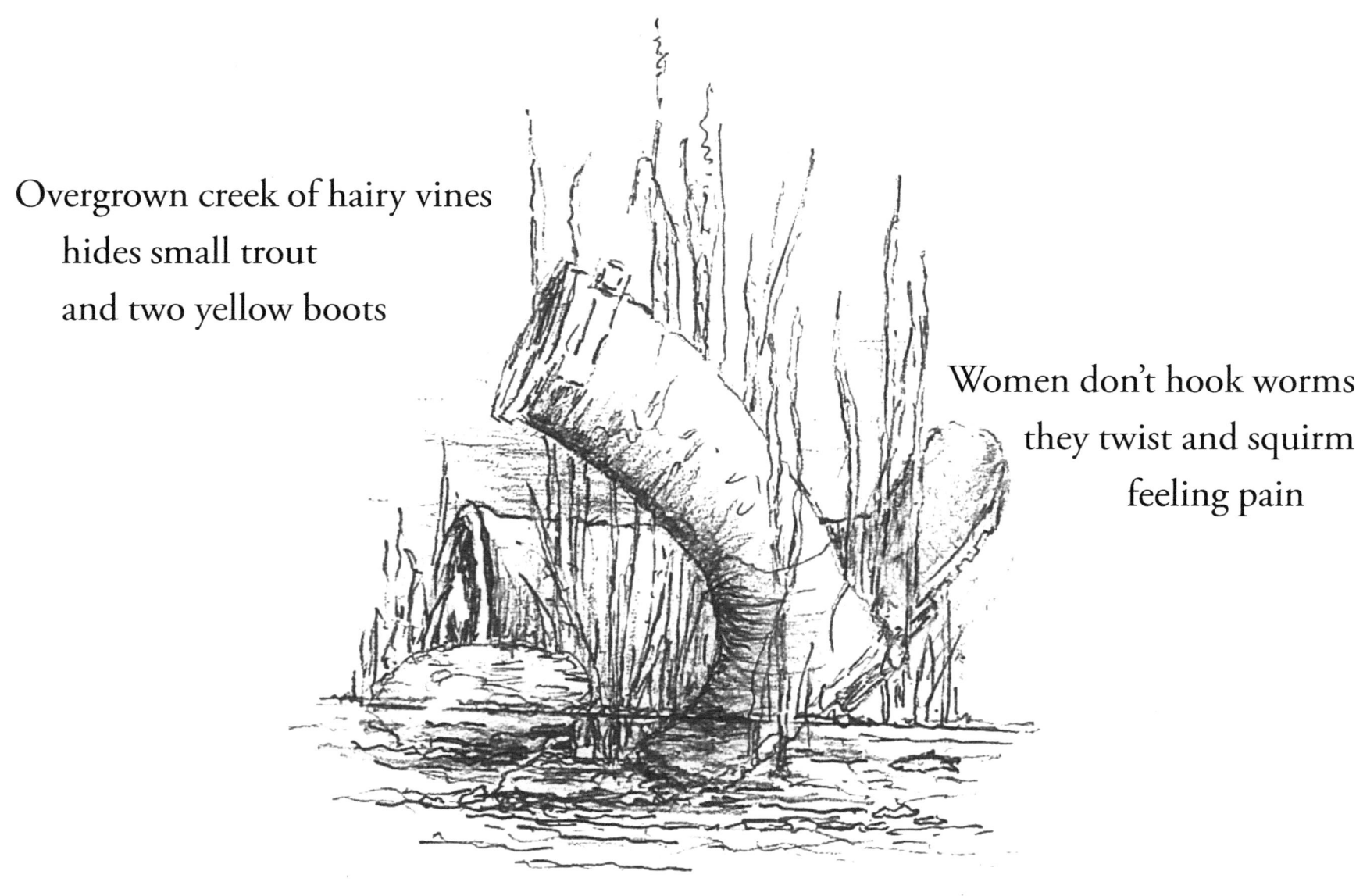

MUSING THE PERSONAL

Red cabin nestled on hilltop
    smoke tails from brick chimney
        my home, sweet home

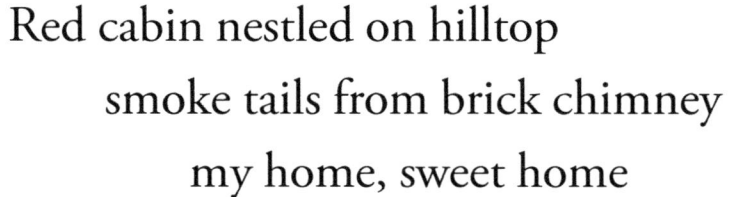

        When family dissolves
    and little good remains
        one fine sister is enough

        Quaint little corner café
    finds me and friend
        sharing espresso

    Teddy bear glowers
        as I leave apartment—
    I am remiss: no goodbye

Billowing clouds
	crash together causing thunder
so said my father long ago

My best fishing pal
stands in waist-high water
me too—a wordless bond

Chain breaks and cross falls
to the grass—quickly I reach
for my life, my all

Awake to bright yellow ceiling
over cozy bed—
	courage for the day

Sitting at my desk
alone and bereft—my muse must be
somewhere else

Watching people go by
I hug hot cup of Joe
on lovely porch café

I like these haiku
but that's no promise
others will too

Candle on my desk/beams more than mere light/an alternate muse

Father says *Don't worry son
hook won't snag you—*
ouch!

Walking along deserted beach
I spy dainty little steps—
ho! where is she?

Girl sitting next to me
in Déjà Vu cafe
sleeps cheek in delicate hand

Father and son in high corn:
    dwell in the land
      and cultivate faithfulness
        (Psalms)

Your heart—
    in all these poems
  I keep reaching for your heart

Life is riven with sorrow
yet bathed in grace and glory

Banana bread in oven
  sweetness fills the room
  my sister, another treat

While memory is a frail guide
  I claim that all manner of thing shall be well

Clouds building overhead
make me think of you
my hurricane

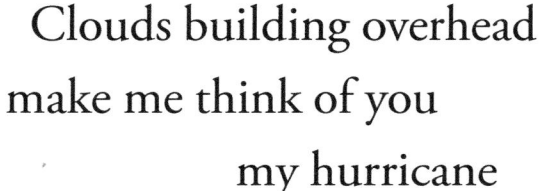

Love
is indeed splendid
except when it's not

OF THE FELINE PERSUASION

Cat tosses catnip
    landing on big belly
suddenly asleep

Amy, my sweet grey cat,
    on backyard fence
        taunts two suitors
    snapping her tail in the air

I sense someone
    peeking in gloomy window
suddenly— it's big boy Tigger!

All day Tigger sleeps/curled in center of my bed/and roams the land all night

Our cunning tabby Moe
    pretends to doze
    sneaky claws

    Tigger in, wild female out—
whatever happened to
    settling turf on their own?

Tiny mouse lies still, silent
while cool cat plays nonchalant—
blink! mouse is away!

Back fence Romeo
    yodels his raucous yowl
        hoping for love

Milk bowl splashes
as tawny kittens
  wade in

Storm has come
    and sleeting rain blinds
  even Master Moe

Red feather
    sticks to Tigger's jowl
  a good night hunting

Amy naps on her back
    and slyly longs for a rub
already the purring

Sitting in backyard
    lost kitten bounces up
      I shout—Theresa!

Leaving bedroom window open
    for Tigger at night
what!— racoons!

        Backyard melody
     and Amy bolts upright
    sniffs, resumes nap

      After long vacation
           kitty sleeps nightly
       on my chest

New plant sits on sill
olive leaves tumble down
where kittens play

Grungy grey tom cat
creeps into alley
beneath pale lamp light

Mother catches Theresa
in the fridge door—
together they cling and cry

Feline HIV took
Tigger's little brother—
vet gave me ten minutes

Pulling car out of parking lot
  I freak at scene in mirror—
    baby Amy on rear window

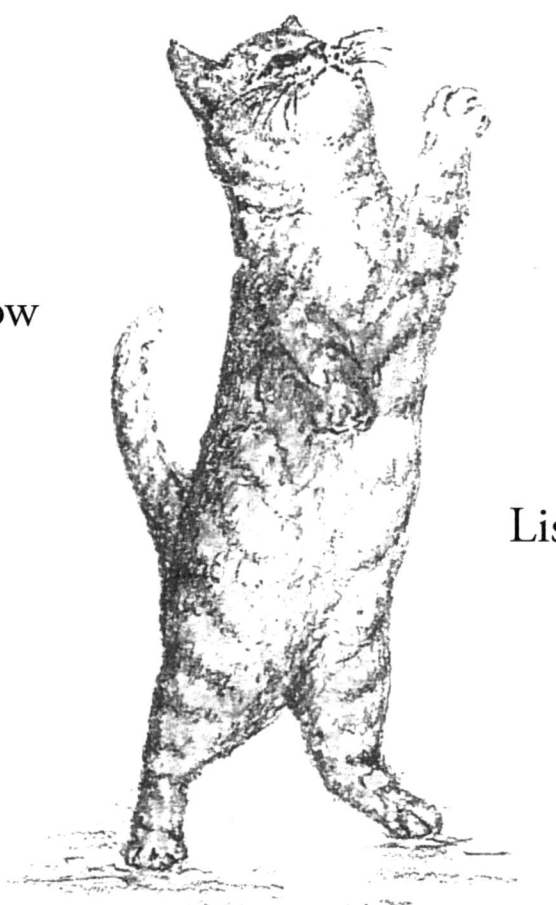

Home from work
Lisa reaches on hind legs
  to nip my nose

Mother lies on side/as kittens push and pull/yummy dinnertime

JUST BECAUSE

Fine old men playing chess
and smoking in the park
they shout, slap their thighs

Twenty-eight faithful folk
gather in small white church:
holy, holy, holy Lord

Soap tied to twine
hanging from sleek faucet
ominous bath looms

Who knows
where to wind goes
surely no one here below
and what of its beginning?

Ballerina on toe
floats over stage
   in ethereal bliss

Hat tilted just so
on his scruffy angled head
he is a world of cool

Cell phones
chatter in dentist's waiting room
inside the drill

The purpose of speech
   is to convey information
but more, love

Pastel spinnakers fill horizon
　　　posing in another world
　while here we yearn

In a dream
Jesus took away my computer
and smiled

Without secrets/our solitude is impugned/but who keeps secrets?

Frog Pond restaurant
serves eggs benedict
with grits on the side

Old woman with walker
limps halfway through crossing
and freezes

Chatty women
   crowd the table
      playing Dominoes

Beethoven's Violin Concerto
   is so exquisite
      he wrote no other

Jesus
stretches out hand to hungry
   seeking daily bread

Boy carries flowers
   to new girl on the block
      see his cheeks!

  Lovely little girl
walking by café—
  yip-yip on leash

Good man Ken
  married a Russian girl
and then he died

Mist on river
  blankets coal barge
  in the west

  Men used to wear suits and ties
  all the time
    now we're bums

  While I'm gone
a neighbor waters plants
and murders a fine one

Heartache
is not required
to write haiku

ABOUT THE AUTHOR

Robb Hasencamp is a Catholic writer who graduated from the Southern Baptist Seminary, Illinois, with an MDiv in theology and psychology. He has lived and worked in Tallahassee; Washington, DC; Seattle; and Miami. His focus has been on corporate training and executive consulting, psychotherapy, and directing social service programs, notably a heroin detox center. His first novel, *Jonathan,* was published in 2020. He now happily lives in St. Petersburg, Florida, where fishing is his favorite pastime.

ABOUT THE ARTIST

Phillippa "Pippa" Francq drew a rabbit at age five and garnered high praise from a mother who painted watercolors. Her early formal art training was in England, with additional art history studies after she came to live in the United States. This background inspired a lifetime of mixed media exploration. Her move into illustrating *Modern American Haiku* is her most recent exciting adventure. Pippa lives in Portsmouth, New Hampshire.

www.ingramcontent.com/pod-product-compliance
Lightning Source LLC
Chambersburg PA
CBHW050847010526
44107CB00017BA/1206